"Don't cry because it's over, smile because it happened."
— Dr. Seuss

"In three words I can sum up everything I've learned about life: it goes on."
— Robert Frost

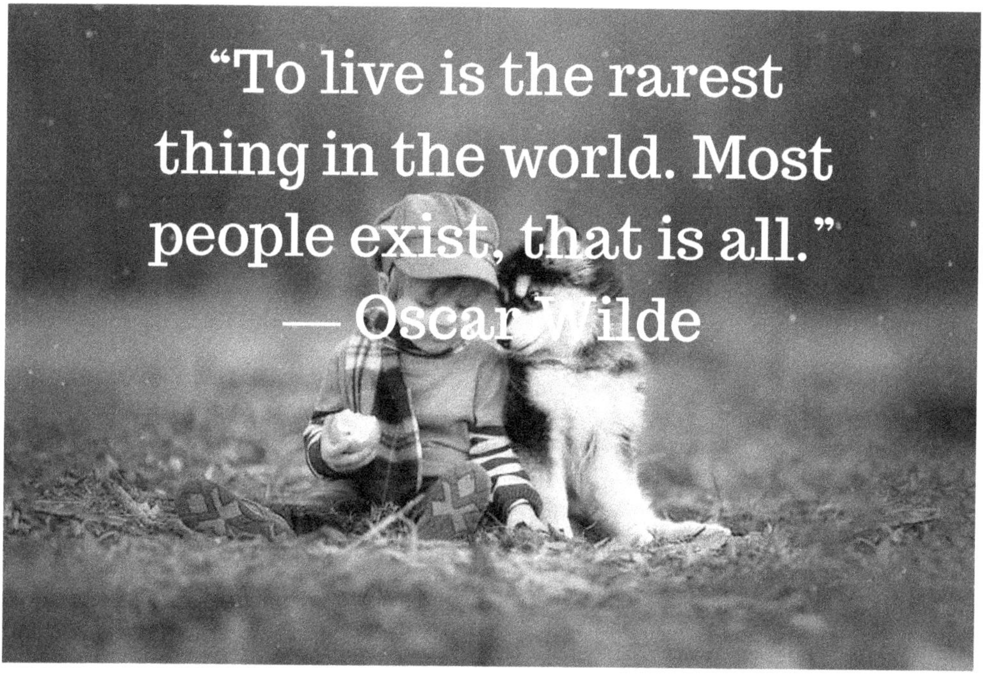

"To live is the rarest thing in the world. Most people exist, that is all."
— Oscar Wilde

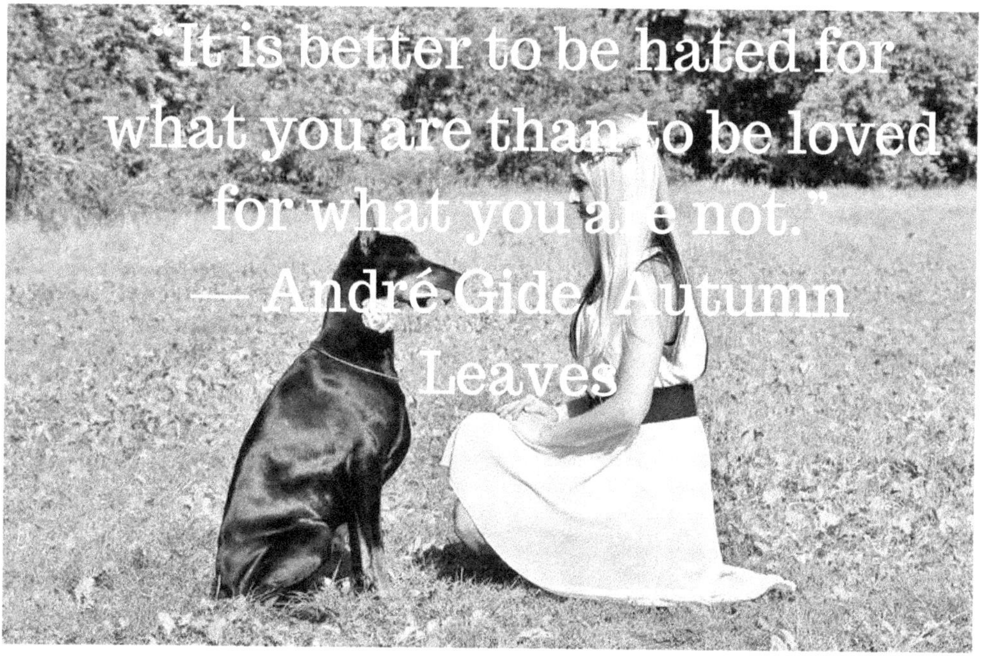

"It is better to be hated for what you are than to be loved for what you are not."
— André Gide, Autumn Leaves

"Insanity is doing the same thing, over and over again, but expecting different results."
— Narcotics Anonymous

"It is better to be hated for what you are than to be loved for what you are not."
— André Gide, Autumn Leaves

"There are only two ways to live your life. One is as though nothing is a miracle. The other is as though everything is a miracle."
— Albert Einstein

"It does not do to dwell on dreams and forget to live."
— J.K. Rowling, Harry Potter and the Sorcerer's Stone

"Good friends, good books, and a sleepy conscience: this is the ideal life."
— Mark Twain

"Life is what happens to us while we are making other plans."
— Allen Saunders

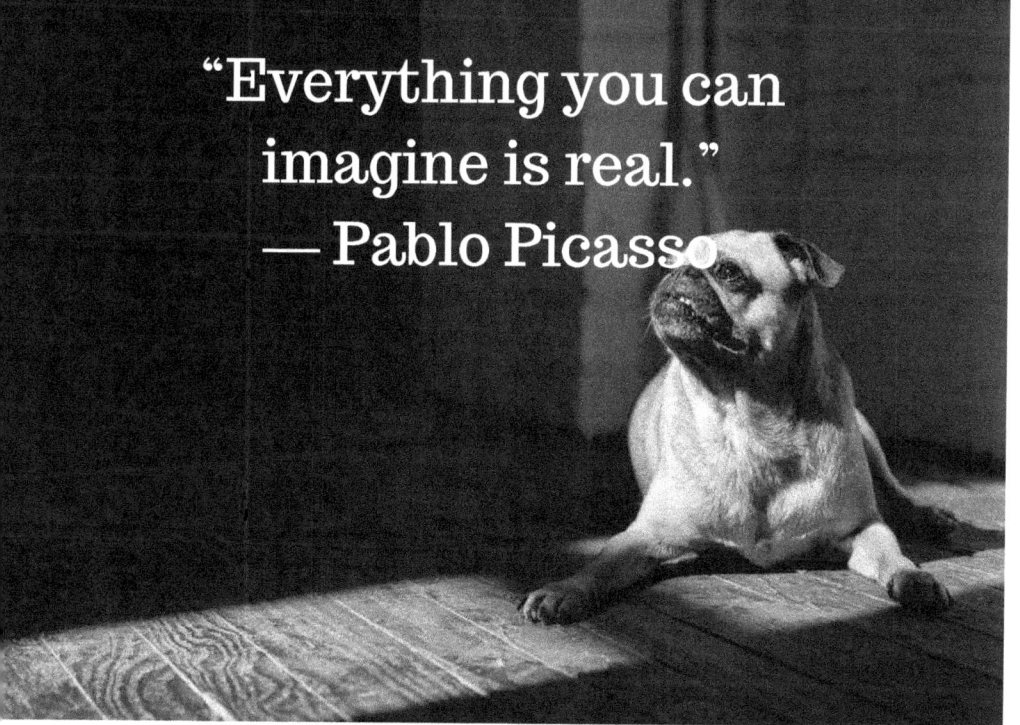

"I may not have gone where I
intended to go, but I think I have
ended up where I needed to be."
— Douglas Adams, The Long
Dark Tea-Time of the Soul

"Everything you can
imagine is real."
— Pablo Picasso

"Today you are You, that is truer than true. There is no one alive who is Youer than You." — Dr. Seuss, Happy Birthday to You!

"I'm not afraid of death; I just don't want to be there when it happens." — Woody Allen

"Life isn't about finding yourself. Life is about creating yourself."
— George Bernard Shaw

Some infinities are bigger than other infin
— John Green, The Fault in Our Stars

"Life is like riding a bicycle. To keep your balance, you must keep moving."
— Albert Einstein

"Reality continues to ruin my life."
— Bill Watterson, The Complete Calvin and Hobbes

"Things change. And friends leave. Life doesn't stop for anybody."
— Stephen Chbosky, The Perks of Being a Wallflower

"The only way out of the labyrinth of suffering is to forgive."
— John Green, Looking for Alaska

"When someone loves you,
the way they talk about you
is different. You feel safe
and comfortable."
— Jess C. Scott, The Intern

"I'm the one that has got to die
when it's time for me to die,
so let me live my life the way
I want to."
— Jimi Hendrix, Jimi Hendrix
- Axis: Bold as Love

"But better to [be] hurt by the truth than com[forted] with a lie."
— Khaled Hoss[eini]

"Just when y[ou] think it can't g[et any] worse, it can. [A]nd just when you think it can't get any better, it can."
— Nicholas Sparks, At First Sight

"We are what we pretend to be, so we must be careful about what we pretend to be."
— Kurt Vonnegut, Mother Night

"The fear of death follows from the fear of life. A man who lives fully is prepared to die at any time."
— Mark Twain

"The one you love and the one who loves you are never, ever the same person."
— Chuck Palahniuk, Invisible Monsters

"I speak to everyone in the same way, whether he is the garbage man or the president of the university."
— Albert Einstein

"We're all human, aren't we? Every human life is worth the same, and worth saving."
— J.K. Rowling, Harry Potter and the Deathly

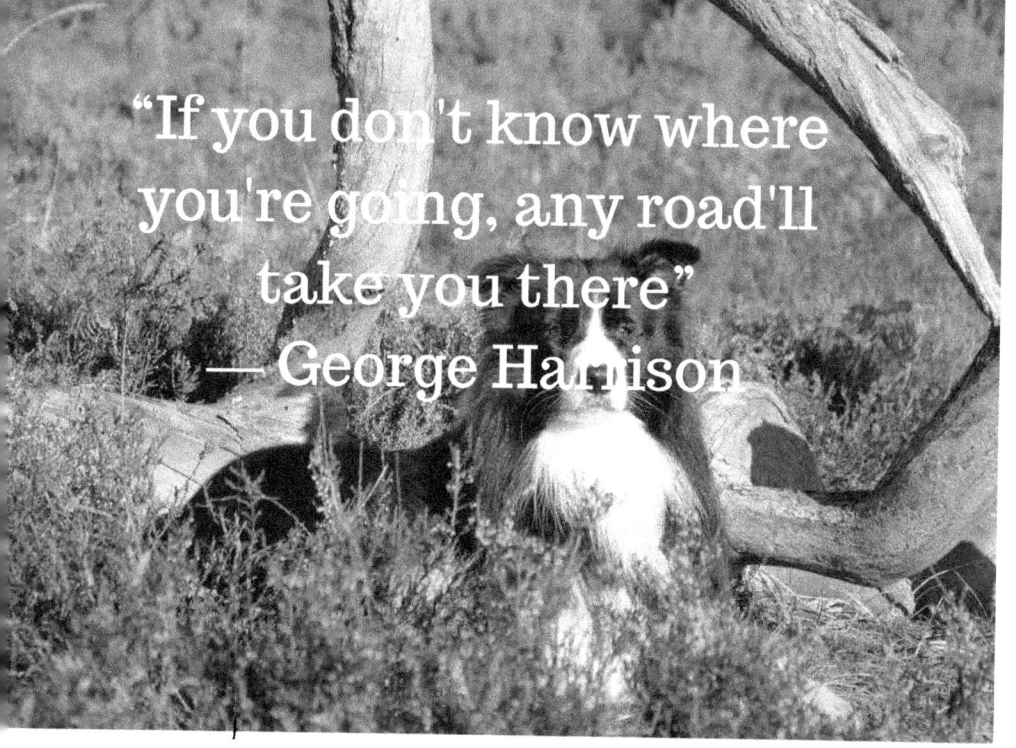

"If you don't know where you're going, any road'll take you there"
— George Harrison

www.ingramcontent.com/pod-product-compliance
Lightning Source LLC
Chambersburg PA
CBHW072034230526
45468CB00021B/1784